BUG
DICTIONARY
An A to Z of Insects and Creepy Crawlies

KU-632-833

Copyright © 2015 Alligator Publishing Limited,
2nd Floor,
314 Regents Park Road,
London N3 2JX,
England

All rights reserved. No part of this publication may be reproduced,
stored in a retrieval system, or transmitted in any form or by any
means electronic, mechanical, photocopying, recording, or otherwise,
without the permission of the copyright holder.

ISBN 978-0-85726-711-5

Printed in China 0194

Size Comparison Pictures

Throughout *Bug Dictionary* you will see a symbol,
either an eye or a hand, next to a small red icon of
each bug listed. The eye or hand will help you to
imagine the size of each bug in real life.

1 in. (25 mm)

The first symbol is a human
eye, which measures about
1 inch (25 mm) across in
real life. Many bugs are
smaller than this, so the size
comparison will help show just
how tiny they can be.

7 in. (175 mm)

The second symbol is a human
adult's hand. This measures
about 7 inches (175 mm) from
the wrist to the tip of the
longest finger. The symbol will
help you to imagine the size of
some of the really big bugs in
this book.

BUG
DICTIONARY
An A to Z of Insects and Creepy Crawlies

www.alligatorbooks.co.uk

Bugs

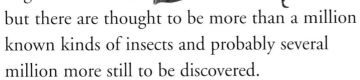

Bugs can be found everywhere! No one has ever been able to count all the bugs in the world, but there are thought to be more than a million known kinds of insects and probably several million more still to be discovered.

Bugs can crawl, run, jump, fly, and even swim. They don't have a backbone or other bones like larger animals. Instead, they are covered in a hard outer skeleton, called an exoskeleton.

Fact

Bugs eat almost every imaginable thing, from carpets to human blood. Many feed on the sweet sugary nectar in flowers. Others are fierce hunters, injecting poison into their victims. Some bugs, such as lice, ticks, and fleas, live on other animals, nibbling at their skin or sucking their blood.

Around Forever

Bugs have been around for a very long time. The first joint-legged animals appeared over one billion years ago in the ocean. The first land-dwelling bugs probably lived 395 million years ago—there are fossils of tiny mites from this time. Scorpions crawled out of the sea about 350 million years ago, and spiders are almost as old.

Fossils of flying insects have been found in rocks 300 million years old. At that time the world was warmer, and large areas of land were covered in vast swampy jungles. Some of the bugs in the swamps were very large. There were giant millipedes (1), giant cockroaches (2), and giant dragonflies (3) with a wingspan of up to three feet.

Bug Groups

Insects – An insect's body is divided into three parts: a head, a thorax, and an abdomen. The head tells the insect about the world around it. It has a mouth, eyes, and a pair of feelers. The thorax is the middle part, where the legs and wings are attached. An insect has three pairs of legs, and an adult insect may have one or two pairs of wings. The abdomen contains the stomach and the insect's other organs.

Spiders, scorpions, ticks, and mites – Unlike insects, spiders and their allies have bodies made up of only two parts, with four pairs of legs, not three.

Millipedes and centipedes – These creatures have flexible bodies made up of lots of little sections, each with one or two pairs of legs.

Fact

Grubs or caterpillars eat and eat until they can't grow any bigger. Then an extraordinary thing happens. The grub grows a hard case around itself and is now called a pupa. Inside the case, all the grub's tissues and organs break down into a kind of soup. Out of this soup, a completely new adult insect forms.

Baby Bugs

Most bugs attract mates by their smell, color, or even by waving their legs or dancing! A few insects, such as aphids, can multiply without mating. Baby bugs that are tiny versions of their parents are called nymphs. Others look very different—these young are called larvae. As bugs grow, they shed their exoskeletons so that they can expand—this is called molting. A soft new "skin" forms under the old, then hardens.

Grasshoppers and dragonflies cannot fly when they are babies, but each time they molt, their wings get bigger. These changes in shape are called metamorphosis. The female dragonfly dips her tail into a pond or river to lay her eggs. The larvae then live as underwater hunters.

Fact
Baby butterflies and moths are called caterpillars, baby flies are called maggots, and baby beetles and bees are called grubs.

Aa Ant

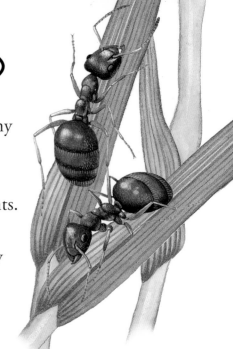

0.2 in. (5 mm)

Ants live deep underground in nests made up of tunnels and rooms. In each colony thousands of ants are ruled by a queen ant, who produces eggs that hatch into worker ants. The workers defend the nest and find food such as scraps of dead animals and plants. They can also attack and kill small insects. When an ant finds a good source of food it leaves a scent trail on its way back to the nest for others to follow. There are about one million trillion ants in the world!

Aphid

0.05 in. (1.25 mm)

Aphids feed on plant sap, piercing stems and sucking up the sweet juice. They multiply rapidly without mating—simply by giving birth to identical babies that are born ready to start feeding. Each female produces up to 100 young, and there may be 20 generations a year.

Army Ant

1 in. (25.4 mm)

Army ants are fierce hunters. Colonies containing as many as 150,000 ants swarm across the forest floor, killing anything in their path. From time to time they rest in a vast mass of ants while the queen ant, safe in the middle, lays her eggs.

Assassin Bug

The assassin bug lies in wait for other insects. Special glands in its body give off a strong smell that helps it attract prey, such as beetles, mosquitoes, and millipedes. It pounces on an insect, seizing it with pincerlike front legs. Next, it injects the victim with deadly saliva that dissolves its insides so the assassin bug can drink them!

0.74 in.
(19 mm)

Fact

Some assassin bugs have a painful bite, and have been called kissing bugs because of their habit of biting people on the lip!

Wingspan
11.8 in. (300 mm)

Atlas Moth

The atlas moth lives in the jungles of southern Asia. With a wingspan of over 11 inches (30 cm), it is one of the largest moths in the world, even bigger than some of the birds in the rain forest. Despite its colorful markings, it blends in well in the flickering light and shade of the forest. Its body, wings, and legs are covered with tiny scales. When the moth is touched, the scales rub off like fine dust.

Bb Backswimmer

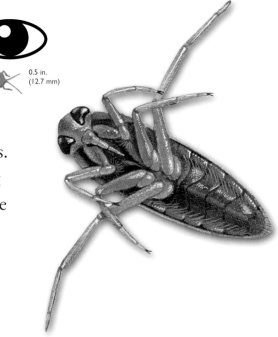

0.5 in.
(12.7 mm)

The backswimmer lives in ponds, lakes, and streams. It lies on its back and rows itself along with paddlelike legs. When underwater, it carries a supply of air under its wings. It feeds on insects, tadpoles, and small fish, sucking out their insides with its beak. To attract a mate, the male backswimmer makes a very loud noise by rubbing his front legs together. You can hear him 130 feet (40 m) away under water.

Wingspan
1.3 in. (33 mm)

Bagworm

The bagworm moth's young larva lives in a large case made of pieces of leaf, twig, bark, and soil, all bound together with silk. The larva crawls around using only its front legs. When it is ready to turn into a moth, it attaches the end of the case to a leaf or twig. Female bagworm moths have no wings, and resemble worms. They stay in or on the case they grew up in, giving off a scent to attract the flying males. After mating, they lay their eggs inside the case.

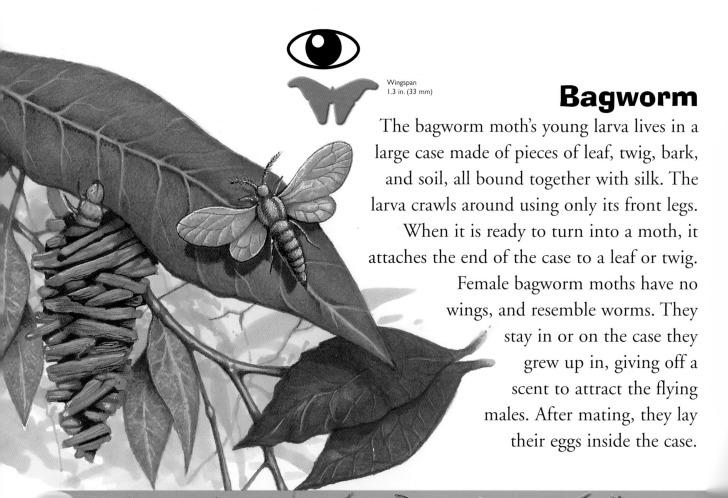

Bedbug

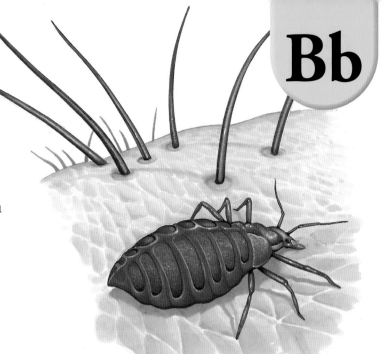

0.3 in. (7.6 mm)

The bedbug hides in dark corners during the day, then comes out at night to feed on human blood. It injects its victim with saliva that prevents the blood from clotting while it feeds—afterwards the skin itches terribly. After a good meal, a bedbug can survive for up to a year without food, but most feed at least once a week.

Black Widow

0.4 in. (10 mm)

The red hourglass pattern on the black widow's abdomen is a sign of danger. She has an extremely painful and sometimes fatal bite. The spider's poison paralyzes the breathing system. To her mate, she is even more dangerous. Male black widow spiders may be eaten by the much larger female after mating—hence the name black widow. Even if he is not eaten, the male usually dies within a day or so from the effort of mating.

Bb Bluebottle

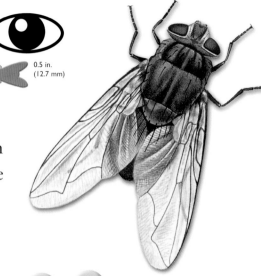

The bluebottle feeds and lays its eggs on rotting meat and dung. It often picks up germs on its feet, and can carry diseases to humans when it lands on their food. The bluebottle's wings can beat up to 200 times a second, 20 times faster than the fastest movement a human can make.

0.5 in. (12.7 mm)

Fact

The bluebottle and other flies taste with their feet, which are 10 million times more sensitive than our tongues.

0.3 in. (7.6 mm)

Bolas Spider

The bolas spider hunts at night by luring moths to it with a special scent. It spins a very sticky ball of silk at the end of a long thread, called a bolas. When a moth comes within reach, the spider whirls the bolas around and around until it hits the moth and sticks to it. Then the spider reels in the moth like a fisherman pulling in a fish.

Bombardier Beetle

The bombardier beetle (right) blasts very hot chemicals at its enemies. When the beetle is threatened, it mixes two chemicals in a special reaction chamber inside its belly—the chemicals reach temperatures of up to 212°F (100°C). The gas squirts out in a tiny puff of smoke, which the beetle aims very accurately by twisting its tail. It can fire off 20 explosions a minute.

0.5 in. (12.7 mm)

Bulldog Ant

1.3 in. (33 mm)

The bulldog ant of Australia (left) is one of the largest ants in the world at up to 1¼ inches (33 mm) long. It has very large jaws with lots of sharp teeth, like a bulldog. It hunts insects and stings them to death.

Bumblebee

The bumblebee has a long, tubelike tongue to suck the sweet, sugary liquid called nectar found deep inside flowers. It will use the nectar to make honey in its underground nest. Pollen from the flower sticks to the hairs on the bee's body, and special combs on its legs scrape the pollen into bristly pollen baskets on its hind legs. Each spring the queen bumblebee builds wax cells and lays eggs in them. The eggs hatch into worker bumblebees, who help build new cells, gather food, and raise new young.

1.6 in. (40 mm)

Cc

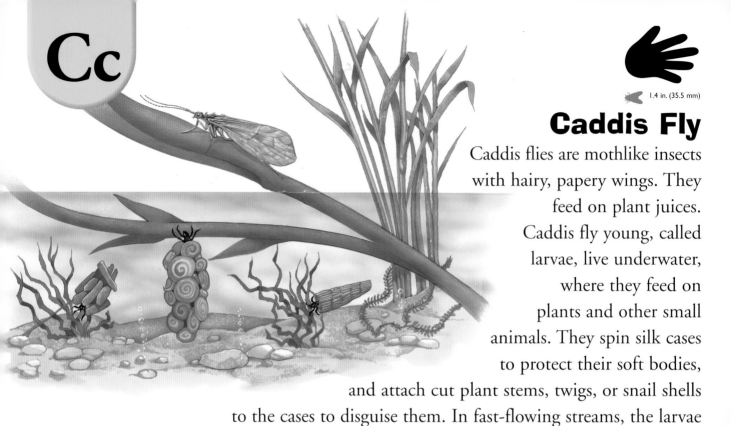

1.4 in. (35.5 mm)

Caddis Fly

Caddis flies are mothlike insects with hairy, papery wings. They feed on plant juices. Caddis fly young, called larvae, live underwater, where they feed on plants and other small animals. They spin silk cases to protect their soft bodies, and attach cut plant stems, twigs, or snail shells to the cases to disguise them. In fast-flowing streams, the larvae attach stones to their silk cases so they are not washed away.

Carpet Beetle

0.2 in. (5 mm)

Carpet beetle larvae, which look like fuzzy worms, can do a lot of damage to carpets, rugs, and clothing. They can destroy stored skins and furs, and even stuffed animals and birds in museums. Unlike the larvae, the tiny adult beetles are harmless, and feed on pollen. In nature, carpet beetle larvae help break down the bodies of dead animals—they can digest fur, feathers, nails, claws, and even hooves!

Carrion Beetle

Carrion beetles are sometimes called sexton beetles or burying beetles because they bury dead animals. The carrion beetles dig away soil beneath a dead animal, so that it sinks deeper and deeper into the soil. The soil eventually falls in on top of the animal and it disappears from view. In a tunnel next to the dead animal, the carrion beetles lay their eggs. Their larvae feed on the rotting flesh of the animal, increasing in weight one hundred times in just a week, and soon change into adult beetles.

0.8 in. (20 mm)

Fact

The male cicada's song is the loudest noise made by any animal—up to 112 decibels, almost as loud as a jet engine. A thin area on the cicada's middle has little ridges, which it rubs together to make the noise. The abdomen acts as an amplifier. To avoid being deafened, the cicada switches off its own hearing organ while it "sings."

1.5 in. (38 mm)

Cicada

(SICK ay duh)

Cicadas feed on plant juices. Young cicadas have no wings and often live underground, where they suck juices from roots. As they grow they shed their skins from time to time, until finally the fully winged adult emerges. Periodical cicadas may spend 17 years as underground grubs, but the adults live for only a few weeks, flying around in search of a mate.

Cc

Click Beetle

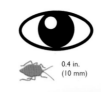

0.4 in. (10 mm)

The click beetle is named for its habit of clicking when it is picked up. If frightened, the beetle rolls onto its back and pretends to be dead. To get back on its feet, it has a clever way of jackknifing into the air, which has earned it the nickname skipjack.

Fact
The click beetle can flick itself 12 inches (30 cm) into the air and land on its feet! It bends its head forward and flicks its body up into the air, twisting around as it goes.

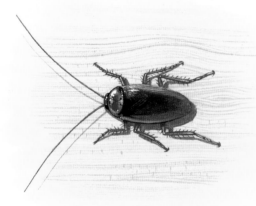

1.4 in. (35.5 mm)

Cockroach

Cockroaches live just about everywhere that humans live. They live in warm, damp, dark places and feed on anything starchy—food scraps, dead insects (including other cockroaches), paper, and clothing. They leave behind them a trail of sticky fluid with a horrible smell.

Cricket

5.9 in. (150 mm)

At rest, the bush cricket looks like a dead leaf, but if frightened it will fly away, displaying a pattern on its wings that looks like the big eyes of a much larger animal—this is to frighten its enemies. The male cricket can rub together special areas at the base of his wings to produce a song. Other crickets listen using ears on their front legs.

Damselfly

Damselflies may be graceful fliers with shimmering colors, but they are also fierce hunters of other insects. When mating, the male damselfly holds the female behind her head and carries her through the air. He supports her in the air while she lays her eggs on underwater plant stems. They will hatch into underwater larvae that hunt small water creatures, including fish.

Wingspan
4.9 in.
(125 mm)

1.4 in. (35.5 mm)

Deathwatch Beetle

The deathwatch beetle lives in tree trunks, wooden furniture, and the old timbers of houses and churches, feeding on the wood itself. In the mating season, the male beetle knocks his head loudly on the wood to attract a female. The beetle's gloomy name comes from people who say the knocking means there will soon be a death in the family.

Dd

Desert Locust

The desert locust (right) is the most destructive insect in the world. It can eat its own weight in food every day. It lives in the dry parts of Africa, the Middle East, and Asia. Huge swarms move across the land, devouring every green thing in their path. The largest swarm ever recorded covered 1,236 square miles (3,200 sq km) and contained 250 billion locusts.

3.5 in. (89 mm)

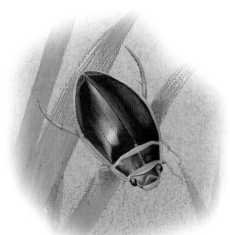

Diving Beetle

1.0 in. (25 mm)

The diving beetle (left) lives in ponds and lakes. It stores bubbles of air under its wing cases, which give it a silvery appearance. From time to time it returns to the water's surface to take in air through the tip of its abdomen. It spends most of the time hunting insects and other small water creatures. Its larva is also a fierce hunter, nicknamed the water tiger.

Dragonfly

Wingspan 3.8 in. (96.5 mm)

Dragonflies are flying killers, catching other insects up to twice their own weight in flight. They are among the fastest flying insects, and can exceed 20 miles (32 km) per hour. Dragonflies are flying acrobats, capable of taking off backwards, hovering, somersaulting, and even stopping dead in the air!

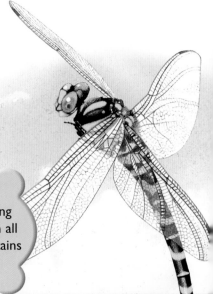

Fact

Dragonflies have amazing eyesight. They can see in all directions. Each eye contains up to 20,000 lenses.

Dung Beetle

Dung beetles feed on dung. They roll it into balls, which they bury underground so they can feed in safety. This also preserves the dung for a long time— out in the air it would rot quickly. Dung beetles roll their dung balls backwards, pushing them with their hind legs. The female beetle lays eggs in the dung ball, so her young will have plenty of food.

1.2 in. (30 mm)

Dung Fly

0.35 in. (8.9 mm)

The dung fly gathers in large numbers on dung, especially on cow patties, to mate. They lay their eggs in the dung and the young fly larvae feed on it, helping to break it down. When they are not busy mating, the flies sit on plants near the dung and attack other flies, breaking their necks before sucking out their juices.

Ee

Earwig

0.6 in.
(15.2 mm)

Earwigs get their name from the idea—which isn't true—that they crawl into people's ears while they are sleeping. Earwigs feed mainly on plant material. They have sharp pincers that can give you a nasty pinch if you try to pick them up. The female curls around her eggs to protect them.

Wingspan
3.35 in.
(85 mm)

Eyed Hawkmoth

When at rest with its wings closed, the eyed hawkmoth is hard to see, because its brown pattern blends with the bark on the tree trunk where it sits. If disturbed, it opens its wings to reveal a startling pair of large eyelike patterns that often frighten away an attacker, who thinks they are the eyes of a much larger animal. While its enemy recovers from the shock, the moth makes its escape.

Fire Ant

Fire ants are serious pests in North and South America. Every year they sting up to 5 million Americans! The queen fire ant lays up to 200 eggs an hour and may produce 3 million daughters. Swarms of fire ants destroy lawns, damage crops, and swarm over traffic lights and airport lights, putting them out of action.

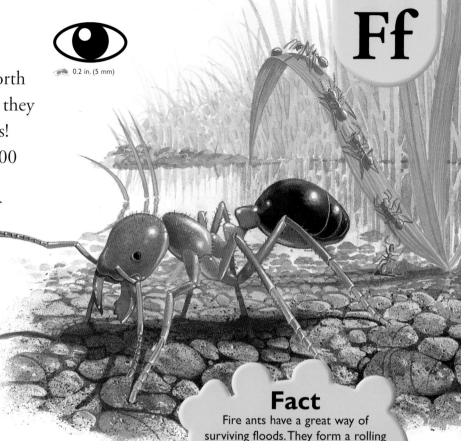

0.2 in. (5 mm)

Ff

Fact

Fire ants have a great way of surviving floods. They form a rolling ball of ants that floats on the water. The ants then take turns to breathe. When they reach something solid they swarm up it.

Fact

There is a very sneaky female firefly that uses the flashing pattern of another kind of firefly. When a male of the other kind comes to her, she grabs hold of him and eats him.

1 in. (25 mm)

Firefly

Fireflies are beetles that produce flashes of light from the tips of their abdomens. They use light to attract a mate. The females stay in one place, while the males try to find them. The pattern of flashing is like a code, telling them whether or not other fireflies are the same species.

Ff

Flea

A flea can leap 130 times its own height. A ball of elastic tissue just above each hind leg is held down by a kind of catch. Release the catch and the flea springs away with incredible speed. Human fleas feed on blood, injecting saliva to prevent the blood from clotting while they feed. The saliva causes intense itching. These and other kinds of fleas have killed millions of people by carrying diseases such as bubonic plague, which killed a quarter of the population of Europe in the 14th century.

0.1 in. (2.5 mm)

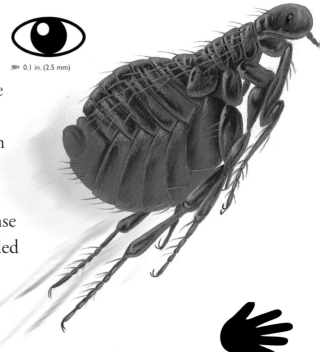

1.56 in. (39.5 mm)

Funnel Web Spider

The funnel web spider of Australia is probably the most dangerous spider on Earth—a bite can kill you! It lives in a silken funnel-shaped web under a stone or log. At night it lies in wait at the entrance of the funnel for passing insects to kill—or a passing foot to bite.

Garden Spider

0.6 in.
(15 mm)

Using silk from the tip of its abdomen, the garden spider spins a web to capture insects for food. Spider silk is extremely strong—a silk thread would have to be over 50 miles (80 km) long before breaking under its own weight. The silk comes out as a liquid which hardens on contact with the air.

Fact

To make a web, first the spider makes a frame of silk threads between some supports, such as twigs. Then it lays down some dry threads that look like the spokes of a bicycle wheel. It makes a spiral of silk to hold these together. Then, walking on the dry threads, it starts to make a new spiral of sticky threads to capture other insects.

0.8 in.
(20 mm)

Glowworm

The glowworm is actually a wingless female beetle. The tip of her abdomen glows to attract a mate. On moonless nights you can see glowworms twinkling in the grass. In the days when there were no electric lights, people used to collect glowworms and arrange them in pretty patterns to make a light show in their gardens.

Gg

5 in.
(127 mm)

Goliath Beetle

The African Goliath beetle is the largest beetle in the world. An adult male may measure over 4.75 inches (120 mm) from the tip of his horn to the end of his body. He is the heaviest insect that is able to fly. Males are very aggressive and often fight with each other, trying to seize the horn of their opponent and throw it into the air.

2.9 in.
(73.5 mm)

Grasshopper

A grasshopper feeds on plants, using its sharp cutting mouthparts. If disturbed, it leaps into the air using its long powerful legs and flies away. When at rest, its colors blend with its background, making it hard to see. Some grasshoppers have brightly colored underwings to startle their enemies and increase their chances of escape.

Fact
Grasshoppers make a kind of buzzing song by rubbing toothlike ridges on their hind legs against raised veins on their front wings. Male grasshoppers sing to attract females and get them to mate.

Harlequin Beetle

The harlequin beetle grows up to 2.75 inches (7 cm) long, with front legs as long as 5.5 inches (14 cm). It feeds on rotting wood and spends its life tunneling into dead tree trunks and fallen logs in the South American jungle. The tunnels let in fungi and other wood-eaters, which help break down the dead wood. Its grublike larvae also live in tunnels in the wood, hidden from predators.

2.75 in. (70 mm)

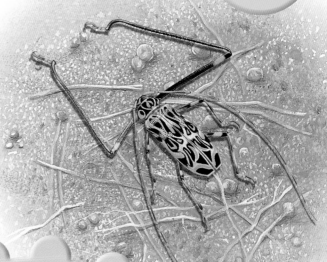

Hh

Fact

When there is plenty of food around, harvester ants gather more seeds than they need. They store the extra food in special chambers in their nests—like a pantry—for times when food is scarce.

0.31 in. (7.8 mm)

Harvester Ant

Harvester ants gather seeds and leaves and store them in their underground nests. They often live in dry regions of the world, where food is in short supply for part of the year. In Arizona's Sonoran Desert, over an area the size of a football field, harvester ants will gather more than 40 million seeds in a year

Hh Honeybee

0.51 in.
(13 mm)

Wild honeybees live in large colonies of thousands of bees. Their nests are found inside hollow trees. The bees feed on nectar, and carry nectar and pollen back to their nest. As they feed, they transfer pollen from one flower to another. If a flower does not receive pollen from another flower, it cannot seed. So without honeybees, humans would have very few food crops.

Fact

The honeybee's nest contains walls of six-sided wax cells. The bees produce the wax from inside their bodies. Some cells contain the bees' eggs and young, while others contain stores of food. The workers are all females and they are ruled by a much larger queen bee, who lays all the eggs.

0.4 in.
(10 mm)

Honeypot Ant

Honeypot ants live in underground nests. Some of the honeypot ants leave the nest to bring back nectar. Other ants waiting at the nest then store the nectar in their bellies—they grow extremely fat and are unable to move very far.

Hornet

1.56 in. (40 mm)

The hornet is a large wasp with a nasty sting and a loud buzz. However, it is a peaceful insect and does not sting unless it is provoked. The hornet lives in a colony of up to 10,000 insects. It builds its papery nest in hollow trees or among the timbers of barns. It feeds on other insects, including wasps and bees.

0.01 in. (0.2 mm)

House Dust Mite

The house dust mite is the cause of much human misery! The mite is a tiny creature that lives in bedding, carpets, and other soft materials. Many humans are allergic to its droppings, which can cause hay fever and asthma (difficulty breathing). Dust mites do some good, however, because they feed on dead skin. Humans shed millions of tiny flakes of skin all the time, which collect invisibly in bedding and mattresses.

Ii

1.4 in. (35.5 mm)

Ichneumon Wasp
(ICK new MAN wasp)

The ichneumon wasp is a parasite, which means it lives and feeds on another animal and gives nothing back in return. The wasp lays her eggs on the grubs of a wood wasp as they lie feeding inside a tree trunk. Somehow the ichneumon wasp knows exactly where the grub is inside the tree. Using a sharp-tipped egg-laying spike she drills through the wood to the grub, then injects her egg. The ichneumon grub will feed on the wood wasp grub, eating it alive.

Fact
The inchworm has the shape and color of a twig, and when not feeding or moving it "freezes." It sticks out from its twig like a little branch so its enemies will not notice it.

Inchworm

2.34 in. (6 mm)

The inchworm is the caterpillar of a geometer moth, whose name means "measuring the earth." The inchworm moves by stretching forward and grasping a twig with its little front legs, then drawing up its rear end with its stubby suckerlike feet. The suckers cling to the twig while the inchworm stretches out again. So it loops along the twig, looking as if it is measuring it inch by inch.

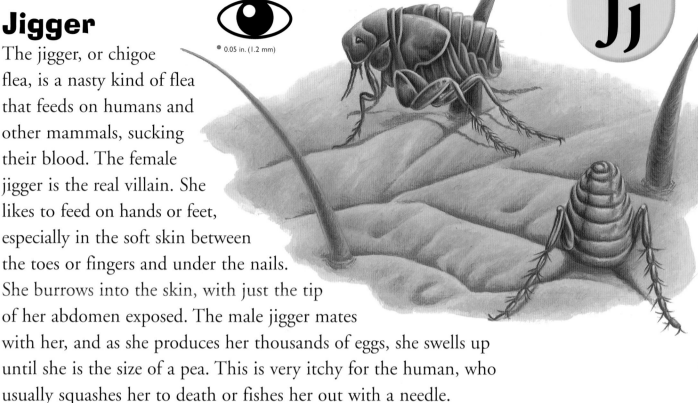

0.05 in. (1.2 mm)

Jigger

The jigger, or chigoe flea, is a nasty kind of flea that feeds on humans and other mammals, sucking their blood. The female jigger is the real villain. She likes to feed on hands or feet, especially in the soft skin between the toes or fingers and under the nails. She burrows into the skin, with just the tip of her abdomen exposed. The male jigger mates with her, and as she produces her thousands of eggs, she swells up until she is the size of a pea. This is very itchy for the human, who usually squashes her to death or fishes her out with a needle.

Female 0.3 in. (7.6 mm)

Jumping Spider

The little jumping spider lies in wait until another insect gets close enough to pounce on. The spider sometimes leaps several times its own length. So, before it jumps, it makes itself a silk lifeline in case it misses and falls. The jumping spider has an amazing lineup of eyes to judge its leap and spot birds and other enemies.

Fact

When a male jumping spider spots a female, he does a kind of dance, waving his brightly colored front legs, wagging his abdomen, and hopping up and down. If the female is interested, she will signal back.

Kk Kallima Butterfly

The kallima butterfly, or dead-leaf butterfly, has a very clever disguise. Can you spot the second butterfly in the picture? When at rest, the butterfly folds its wings together showing the undersides, which look just like a dead leaf. When the butterfly rests at an angle to the stem, it appears to be just another leaf.

Wingspan
3.15 in. (80 mm)

Fact
In the Amazon, there are about 2,000 different species of katydid. Even though they are camouflaged on the trees, their mating calls sometimes give them away and attract hungry birds and bats!

5.9 in. (150 mm)

Katydid

The katydid is a long-horned grasshopper, a kind of grasshopper with very long feelers. Its name comes from the song that it chirps repeatedly, which sounds like "katy did, katy didn't." The katydid sings at night, by rubbing its left front wing against a ridge on the right wing. Many katydids look like green leaves or dead leaves, so their enemies do not notice them.

Lacewing

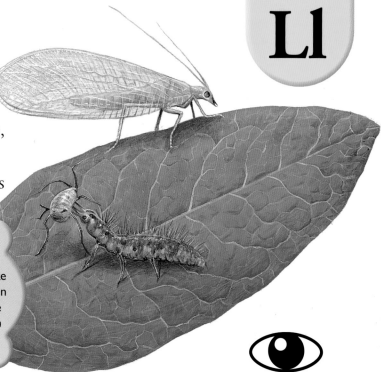

0.6 in. (15 mm)

Despite its fragile beauty, the lacewing is a fierce hunter, catching, killing, and eating insects, pests, and mites. The lacewing larvae hunt smaller insects, and some cover their bodies with the dead bodies of their prey for camouflage.

Fact

Some lacewing larvae are called ant lions. They live in sandy pits like the craters of tiny volcanoes. When another insect falls over the edge of its pit, the ant lion pelts it with sand to stop it from escaping.

0.3 in. (7.6 mm)

Ladybug

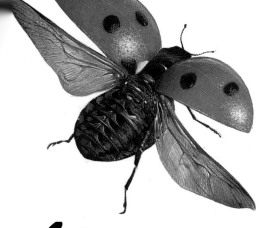

Under its hard red wing cases, the ladybug has a pair of larger, more delicate wings. Ladybugs and their larvae are useful insects because they have a huge appetite for aphids and other pests. Their colorful bodies warn enemies that they taste awful. If the ladybug is faced with a dangerous enemy, it will squeeze out foul-smelling fluid from its knees.

Lantern Fly

3.1 in. (78.5 mm)

The lantern fly is really a big planthopper that feeds on sap. Its large head seems to glow at times, hence its name. When threatened, some lantern flies open their wings and reveal huge eyelike markings on the underwings, as if a large animal is staring at the attacker.

Ll

Leafcutter Ant

The leafcutter ant is a gardener. It cuts off pieces of leaf and carries them back to its underground nest. Lines of leafcutter ants march through the forest, carrying along leaves, seeds, and flowers. In special chambers called fungus gardens, they grow a special fungus on which they feed (the leaves provide food for the fungus to grow). Their underground nests may extend for several yards under the jungle floor.

0.5 in.
(12.5 mm)

Fact
Over a million ants live in a leafcutter nest. They come in several sizes—workers do the leaf-cutting and carrying, soldier ants guard them, while tiny leafcutters ride on the leaves, fighting off attacks from wasps.

4 in.
(101.5 mm)

Leaf Insect

The leaf insect has an interesting camouflage—it looks just like a heap of leaves. Its wings and the sections of its legs each look like a leaf, complete with veins and blotches. Some leaf insects pretend to be green leaves, while others look like dead brown leaves. The insect remains still for long periods of time to increase the effect.

Louse

A louse is a parasite that lives on the body fluids of another living animal. The head louse lives in hair, clinging on with its hooked claws. Its flattened body fits easily between the hairs, where it pierces the scalp and sucks up blood. If a person has a lot of head lice, they can cause itching. The louse glues its tiny eggs, called nits, to the hairs. A fine-toothed comb and special shampoo can help clear lice and nits from hair.

0.1 in. (2.5 mm)

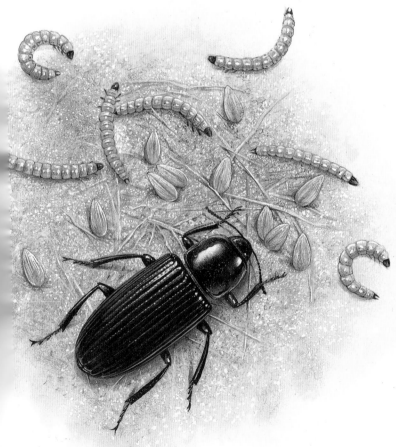

0.5 in. (12.7 mm)

Mealworm

Mealworms are the young wormlike larvae of beetles that feed on dry, starchy food. Fishermen use them as bait, and they make good food for pet snakes, lizards, and frogs. A beetle's eggs hatch into mealworms, which feed and grow until they are big enough to form pupae and turn into adult beetles.

Mm Millipede

11 in. (280 mm)

Millipedes have been around for 400 million years. The name "millipede" means "a thousand legs." But in fact, most millipedes have no more than 200 legs. The number of legs increases as the millipede grows bigger. Some giant tropical millipedes grow up to 11 inches (280 mm) long, while the tiniest ones are only 0.06 inches (2 mm) long. When threatened, a millipede curls into a tight coil, its soft underparts protected by the tough armor plating on its back. Many millipedes also produce a nasty-smelling poisonous liquid or gas to keep their enemies away. Millipedes feed on dead plant material, so they help clean up the environment.

1.8 in. (45.7 mm)

Mole Cricket

The mole cricket lives underground. Like a mole, it has shovel-shaped legs and feet for digging, and a pointed head for pushing through the soil. It feeds on grubs, worms, beetles, and caterpillars, which it finds in its burrows. The male mole cricket digs a burrow with two entrance funnels that act like megaphones to amplify his mating calls.

Monarch

The monarch is a large butterfly with striking orange and black colors. These colors are nature's warning—they advertise that the butterfly and its caterpillars are poisonous. Monarchs feed on milkweed plants and take in the plant's poisons to use for their own defense. If a bird eats the bad-tasting monarch, it will easily recognize another one and avoid it in the future.

Wingspan
4 in.
(101.5 mm)

Fact

Monarch butterflies are powerful fliers and can travel long distances. Canadian monarchs migrate 2,000 miles (3,200 km) south to spend the winter in Florida, Mexico, or California. Some even cross the Atlantic Ocean and turn up in the UK. In Australia the monarch is called "the wanderer."

Morpho

Now you see it—now you don't! The morpho butterfly performs an amazing disappearing act to fool its enemies. When it opens its huge wings, there is a brilliant flash of metallic blue, but when it closes them it seems to disappear. The undersides of the wings have a mottled brown pattern that blends in with the bark of trees. This confuses its enemies as they try to chase it.

Wingspan
6.46 in. (164 mm)

Mm

0.3 in. (7.6 mm)

Mosquito

Mosquitoes split their lives between dry land and water. The female lays a floating raft of eggs on the surface of a pond. The eggs hatch into wrigglers, little wormlike larvae that hang from the water's surface and filter out tiny plants and animals to eat. They breathe through air tubes at the tips of their tails. The male mosquito feeds on nectar, but the female needs a meal of blood to provide protein to make her eggs. She flies from one person to another and can transmit dangerous diseases like malaria, which kills over 3 million people a year. This makes the mosquito the most dangerous insect in the world.

Fact
The female mosquito sucks a tiny drop of blood each time she bites. She will only stop if she is disturbed, or if the nerve from her abdomen tells her she is full. If this nerve is cut, she will keep sucking until she bursts!

Mud Dauber Wasp

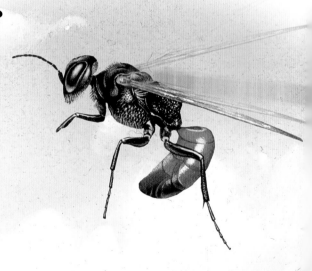

1.5 in. (38 mm)

The mud dauber wasp shapes her nest from balls of mud that she molds with her jaws, forming several cells in which she will lay her eggs. Before laying the eggs, she catches a spider and injects it with a paralyzing poison. Then she drags the spider into a cell and lays an egg on it. The young wasp larvae will feed on the paralyzed spider.

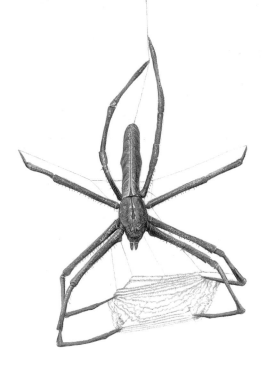

Net-casting Spider

0.78 in. (20 mm)

The net-casting spider makes a strange basket-shaped web. When it gets dark, the spider takes up a position hanging from a twig and holding the web with its front legs close to the ground. When an insect passes below, the spider throws the net over it. Some net-casting spiders are called "ogre-faced" spiders. To judge exactly where to throw their net they have a really huge pair of blue eyes and possibly the most powerful night vision of any small animal.

Nut Weevil

0.3 in. (7.6 mm)

The nut weevil can drill its way into nuts to feed on the soft flesh inside. It has biting jaws right at the tip of its snout that allow it to do this. The weevil's long, curved snout can reach deep inside the nut, so it needs to make only a small hole. Weevils can cause serious damage to crops such as cotton, nuts, and other stored food.

Oo

Oil Beetle

1.24 in. (31.5 mm)

The oil beetle is a strange kind of beetle. It has no hind wings, and its front wings do not meet over its back. It produces a nasty-smelling oily liquid from its joints to make sure its enemies leave it alone. Newborn oil beetle larvae have a remarkable life—they cling to wild bees and are carried to the bees' nests. In the nests, they feed on the bees' grubs and honey.

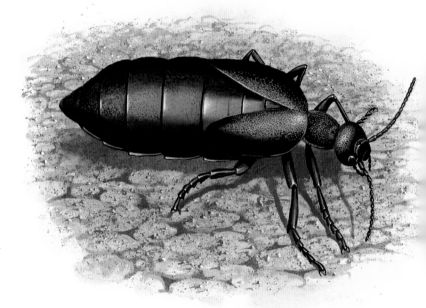

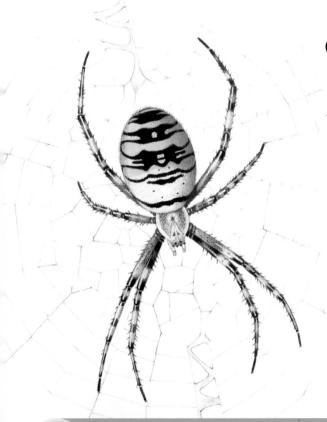

Orb Web Spider

1 in. (25.4 mm)

The orb web spider spins a huge sloppy web up to a yard across— sometimes hanging between two trees or across a stream. At the center of the web is a thick white zigzag structure, probably to alert birds so they don't fly into the web and damage it. The female orb web spider catches large flying insects such as crickets and butterflies. She is very large, but her male partner is tiny—1,000 times lighter. He doesn't spin a web but lives in the female's, trying to avoid being eaten by her before he has had a chance to mate.

Peppered Moth

The peppered moth blends so well with the bark of the trees it lives in that it is hard to spot it. Rarely, plain black peppered moths occur. They are much easier to see and are usually eaten quickly by birds.

Wingspan
2.05 in.
(52 mm)

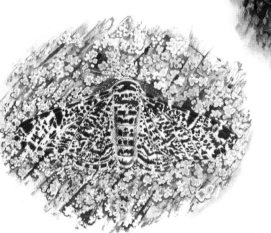

Fact

Years ago, when factories used to produce clouds of smoke, the trees became very blackened. The black variety of peppered moths were well camouflaged on the black bark. Their numbers increased, while the number of mottled brown moths decreased because they got eaten by birds. Today there is much less pollution, so most of the moths that survive are mottled brown ones.

0.75 in.
(19 mm)

Pill Millipede

The pill millipede is a small creature covered with strips of "armor." It scuttles through leaf litter on its many legs, feeding on scraps of dead plant material. When threatened it can roll up into a tight ball, completely enclosed in armor. It also rolls up during a drought, to keep moisture from escaping through its armor.

Praying Mantis

3.5 in. (89 mm)

The praying mantis stays perfectly still as it lies in wait for its prey—holding its front legs together as if it is praying. Even if it decides to stalk its prey, it moves very slowly, one foot at a time. By creeping up on its victim, the mantis also makes itself less obvious to its own enemies. When an insect comes within reach, the mantis flicks out its long front legs with astounding speed to seize it.

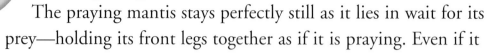

Pseudoscorpion

0.3 in. (7.6 mm)

(SOOD oh SCORE pee on)

The pseudoscorpion, or false scorpion, is a miniature hitchhiker. It often clings to the legs of insects in order to get from one place to another. A true scorpion stings with its tail but a pseudoscorpion attacks prey with its poisonous pincers. Like a true scorpion, it is a hunter and it has a very similar courtship dance, with the male and female grasping each other with their pincers as they dance.

Queen Alexandra's Birdwing

The Queen Alexandra's birdwing is the largest and heaviest butterfly in the world. The biggest one ever found measured over 11 inches (28 cm) from wingtip to wingtip. It is very popular with illegal collectors, and is becoming very rare. These butterflies are difficult to collect because they live in the treetops, so collectors shoot them down with guns loaded with dust or water.

Wingspan
11 in. (280 mm)

Fact

Many spiders that live near water can swim. They do a kind of frog kick with all their legs at the same time, pushing back the water and curling their legs forward ready for another big push.

0.8 in.
(20.3 mm)

Raft Spider

The raft spider is sometimes called the fishing spider. It lives near water and hunts by sitting on a waterweed and resting a foot on the water's surface, where it can detect vibrations coming from insects struggling in the water. It also catches tadpoles and small fish. The female raft spider carries her large egg sac around with her. The sac is made of silk and contains about 40 eggs.

Qq
Rr

Rr

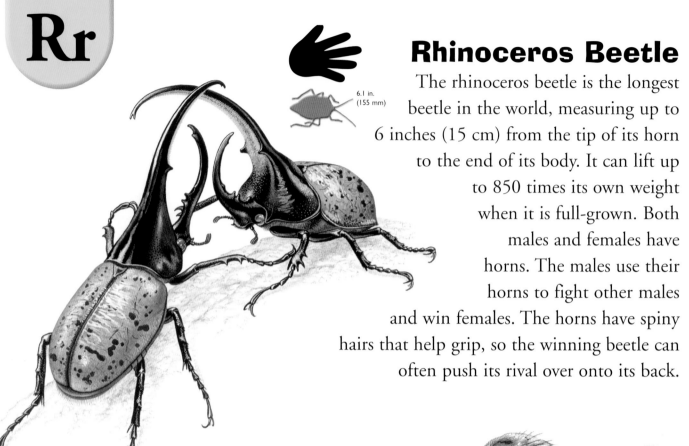

Rhinoceros Beetle

The rhinoceros beetle is the longest beetle in the world, measuring up to 6 inches (15 cm) from the tip of its horn to the end of its body. It can lift up to 850 times its own weight when it is full-grown. Both males and females have horns. The males use their horns to fight other males and win females. The horns have spiny hairs that help grip, so the winning beetle can often push its rival over onto its back.

6.1 in.
(155 mm)

Robber Fly

Also called the assassin fly, the robber fly is a vicious predator. It lies in wait for other insects until they are close enough to pounce on, or it chases them through the air. Once an insect is caught by the robber fly's long, bristly legs, it has no chance of escaping. The robber fly kills it instantly by injecting poison from its beaklike mouth. The fly then injects digestive juices and sucks its victim dry.

1 in.
(25.4 mm)

Fact
Some robber flies look just like certain bees. This allows them to get very close to the bees, making it easier to catch them.

Sand Wasp

1 in.
(25.4 mm)

The female sand wasp
lays her egg in an underground
burrow. First, she captures a big caterpillar
and injects it with poison to paralyze it.
She drags the caterpillar into the
burrow, then lays an egg on it.
The sand wasp's young larva
will feed on the living caterpillar.
The sand wasp carefully closes the burrow with
a stone and arranges other small stones around it to
conceal the entrance, and to help her recognize it again.

Fact

The world's most dangerous
scorpion, called *Androctonus*, lives
in North Africa and Asia. Its poison
can kill a human in 4 hours or a
dog in just 7 minutes!

Scorpion

2.5 in.
(63.5 mm)

Scorpions were
among the first
predators to walk the
earth, some 350 million
years ago. They live in deserts
and other dry places, and come
out at night to hunt. Scorpions use
their large, vicious pincers to capture their prey—mainly insects, spiders,
and other scorpions, although large scorpions eat lizards and mice too.
The most dangerous part of the scorpion is its stinger at the end of its tail.
The scorpion can whip its stinger over its head with lightning speed,
delivering a poisonous sting, which in some species can kill a human.

Ss

2.5 in. (63.5 mm)

Silkworm

The silkworm is the caterpillar of the silkworm moth, which comes from China. The caterpillar feeds on mulberry leaves but may also eat lettuce leaves or other plants. Silkworms have been farmed for their silk for at least 3,000 years. Using special glands that open near its mouth, the caterpillar spins nearly 3,300 feet (1,000 m) of silk thread as it makes its cocoon. Once inside the cocoon, the caterpillar will change into a moth.

Fact

The female silkworm moth lives for only two or three days. During this time she will lay as many as five hundred eggs.

Silverfish

0.5 in. (12.7 mm)

The silverfish is a simple wingless insect covered with silvery scales. It usually lives in houses, hiding from the light—it scuttles quickly across the floors of kitchens and bathrooms, where it feeds on materials like glue, paper, and scraps of human food.

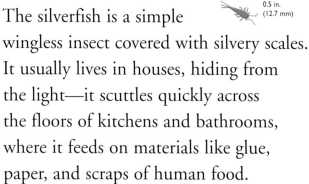

Wingspan
1.25 in. (31.7 mm)

Skipper

Skippers are a kind of cross between a butterfly and a moth. Unlike most butterflies, they rest with their lower wings spread out flat and their upper wings held at an angle. Skippers are named for their rapid, darting way of flying. Despite their small size, they can reach speeds of 18 miles (30 km) per hour.

Spitting Spider

0.3 in.
(7.6 mm)

The spitting spider uses a gluey liquid to catch its prey. When an insect wanders within reach, the spider spits its sticky saliva at the prey, gluing it to the ground. The threads of saliva zigzag over the prey, holding it down so the spider can approach its victim and bite it to death.

Ss Stag Beetle

The huge, antlerlike jaws of male stag beetles are mainly for display—to threaten other beetles or enemies. They don't have much of a bite, but adult stag beetles rarely feed. Their lives are all about finding a female to mate with. When a male meets a rival, the two beetles rear up on their hind legs and try to seize each other in their jaws. The aim is to toss the enemy into the air—or off the tree! The larger beetle usually wins by flipping its rival onto its back, where it finds it hard to get up again.

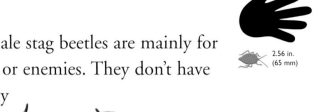

2.56 in. (65 mm)

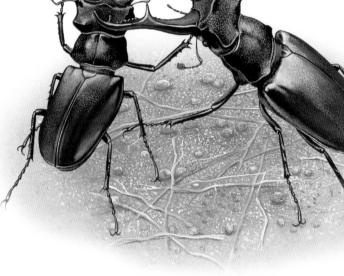

0.33 in. (8.3 mm)

Stalk-eyed Fly

The stalk-eyed fly looks extraordinary because it has a very wide head and its eyes are on stalks. Rival males come head to head and use their eyes to "measure" whether their enemy is bigger and stronger than they are. If his eyes are farther apart, then he must be a bigger fly, so the smaller one retreats!

Stink Bug

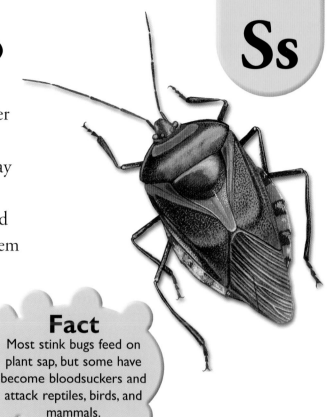

0.2 in. (5 mm)

Stink bugs are called that because they leave a trail of really smelly liquid wherever they go. If the liquid gets on fruit, it gives it a terrible taste. The stink bug's enemies keep away from it because of the smell. Stink bugs are sometimes called shield bugs because they stand guard over their eggs and young, protecting them with their shieldlike bodies.

Fact

Most stink bugs feed on plant sap, but some have become bloodsuckers and attack reptiles, birds, and mammals.

Wingspan 3.94 in. (100 mm)

Swallowtail

The swallowtail butterfly is named for the streamers at the tips of its rear wings. When at rest, the streamers look like feelers and distract enemies from its delicate head. During its caterpillar stage, the swallowtail has an unusual defense against its enemies. A strange-looking forked orange device just behind its head shoots in and out when the caterpillar is frightened, giving off a bad smell.

Tt Tarantula

Tarantulas are some of the world's biggest spiders, up to 8 inches (20 cm) long. They can live for up to 30 years! Despite their scary reputation, they are shy and rarely bite people. Tarantulas are often covered with up to a million prickly hairs that come off when they are touched and hook into the skin. Tarantulas live in burrows in the forest floor, waiting for prey to pass by. A large tarantula may kill small snakes and even birds.

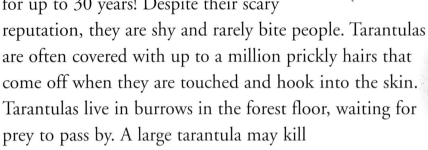

8 in.
(203 mm)

Fact

Termite nests are made of soil and termite saliva. Some are over 25 feet (7.5 m) tall. The nest also reaches deep underground. Inside are lots of tunnels and rooms. The millions of termites give off a lot of heat, but the nest has an amazing cooling system. Tunnels take the heat up into the mound, branching out to the air, so heat is lost.

0.5 in.
(12.7 mm)

Termite

Termites are blind insects similar to big ants. Millions of termites live together in a colony, ruled over by a huge queen who can live for over 50 years. She lives in a special room in the nest, called the royal chamber, together with the king termite. The worker termites attend to all her needs. Many queen termites are so fat and full of eggs that they cannot move.

Tt

Thrips

Thrips are small but irritating insects, which seem to get everywhere—in your eyes, ears, and nose. They are tiny insects, usually no longer than 0.12 inches (3 mm), that feed on plant sap or hunt even tinier creatures. Most thrips have delicate fringed wings and are poor flyers. They can multiply rapidly without mating, especially in warm, dry weather.

0.06 in. (1.5 mm)

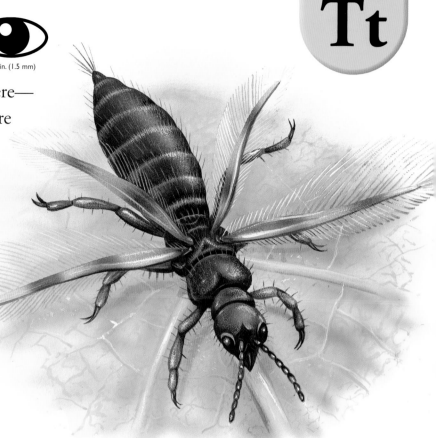

0.125 in. (3 mm)

Tick

Ticks are parasites that live on animals, including humans. After hatching from an egg, a tick will take about three years to grow up. During that time it will feed about once a year. When full-grown, ticks feed on blood, clinging so firmly to skin that they are very difficult to get off. When the tick is full of blood it will drop off.

Tt

Tiger Beetle

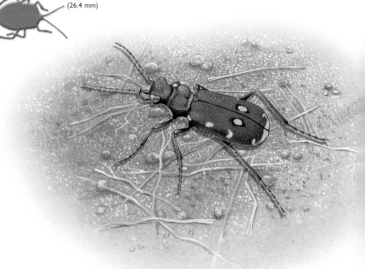

1.04 in. (26.4 mm)

This beetle is a very fierce hunter, just like its namesake, the tiger. It has long legs and can run very fast—even faster than a cheetah—as it chases insects. Its larva is also a hunter. It lives in a hole in the ground, seizing passing prey in its curved jaws. Hooks on its abdomen help it cling to its burrow as it struggles with its prey.

Trapdoor Spider

1.57 in. (40 mm)

Trapdoor spiders live in tubelike burrows lined with silk. To make the trapdoor, the spider cuts around the rim of the tube, leaving one small piece of earth attached like a hinge. It adds extra silk to the lid and hinge to make them stronger and hides the surface with soil and bits of moss. When the spider feels hungry it waits just below the trapdoor until it feels the shudder made by a moving insect. Then it jumps out and pounces on its prey.

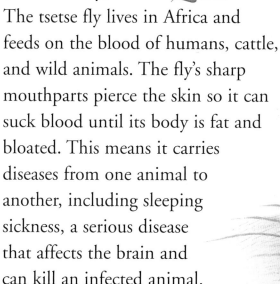

 Treehopper

0.55 in.
(14 mm)

Treehoppers have been around for over 40 million years. They come in many strange shapes and sizes. The treehoppers shown here are shaped like thorns so enemies do not notice them as they suck the sap from a plant stem. The treehoppers sit so that the pointed "thorns" on their backs face the same way as the plant's thorns—this is called mimicry.

Fact

The treehopper produces a sticky substance called honeydew that is collected and eaten by ants. In return for the honeydew, the ants protect the treehoppers from enemies such as spiders.

Tsetse Fly

(t SET see fly)

 0.35 in.
(8.9 mm)

The tsetse fly lives in Africa and feeds on the blood of humans, cattle, and wild animals. The fly's sharp mouthparts pierce the skin so it can suck blood until its body is fat and bloated. This means it carries diseases from one animal to another, including sleeping sickness, a serious disease that affects the brain and can kill an infected animal.

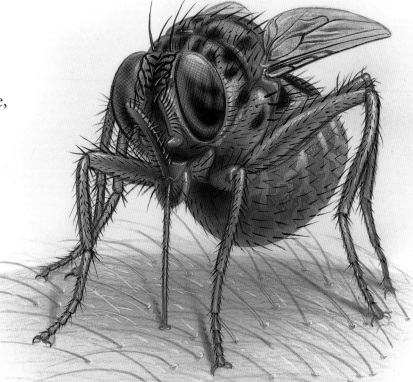

Uu

Underwing Moth

Wingspan
2.28 in.
(58 mm)

The underwing moth uses bright colors to startle its attackers. When threatened, it flashes its brilliantly colored underwings. As its enemy stops in surprise, the moth takes off, making a quick getaway. As soon as the moth lands on a tree trunk, with its underwings hidden again, it blends in with the bark and becomes very difficult to spot.

Uraniid Moth

Wingspan
2.68 in.
(68 mm)

(YOO ran EE idd moth)
The uraniid moth is part of the swallowtail moth family, whose members have wings shaped like swallow's tails. Its wings are brightly colored to warn off enemies. It lives in the jungles of Australia and New Guinea. During the day it visits flowers near the ground, but at dusk it circles high up in the trees.

Velvet Ant

The velvet ant is a wingless female wasp—with a painful sting. When mating, the male clings to the female and flies off with her. Velvet ants are parasites of other wasps. They lay their eggs in other wasps' nests. Their eggs hatch earlier than those of the other wasp, so their larvae feed on the other wasp's food supplies, and then on its larvae.

0.7 in. (17.8 mm)

0.2 in. (5 mm)

Velvet Mite

The giant velvet mite is the largest mite in the world, about the size of a large raisin. It lives underground in the American deserts. It usually comes out in large numbers after the first heavy rainfalls to catch swarms of termites, which are its favorite food.

Ww

Wasp

Wasps have a painful sting, and their bright yellow and black colors are a warning of this. Wasps kill and eat other insects, but they also like nectar and juices from fruit. Paper wasps live in an oval nest made of "paper"—a mixture of wood and saliva. Inside the nest are rows of cells containing the wasp's eggs and young. The strongest female paper wasp takes the role of queen, bullying the others so they don't lay eggs or grow as big as she is.

0.8 in.
(20 mm)

Fact
If the temperature inside a wasps' nest is too cold, the wasps pump their wing muscles without moving their wings—this produces heat. If the nest is too hot, the wasps bring in droplets of water, which evaporate and cool the air.

1 in.
(25.4 mm)

Water Scorpion

With strong curving front legs for grabbing prey, the water scorpion looks similar to a desert scorpion. Its tail does not have a stinger like a scorpion's—it has a pair of breathing tubes instead. The water scorpion hunts upside down, keeping its breathing tubes at the water's surface to take in air. It is not a very good swimmer, so it lies very still and waits for its prey.

Water Spider

The water spider spends most of its time inside a bell-shaped web attached to underwater plants. It swims up and down to the water's surface, carrying air trapped under the hairs on its belly to fill its bell. Then it lurks at the entrance to its home, waiting for prey to come within reach.

0.5 in.
(12.7 mm)

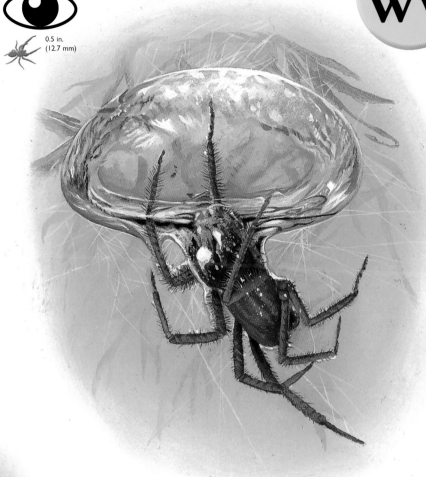

Water Stick Insect

2.15 in. (54.6 mm)

Disguised as a stick, the water stick insect stays very still and waits among the water weeds until a water flea or tadpole comes within its reach. Then it flicks out its long front legs and seizes its prey. The water stick insect has a painful sting, which it will use if touched or threatened.

Ww Weaver Ant

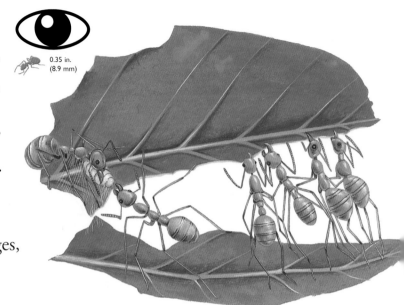

0.35 in.
(8.9 mm)

Weaver ants live in leafy shelters up in the trees. The shelters are made by folding leaves and gluing them together. The ants' young larvae produce the silky glue. Some ants then hold the leaves in place, while others swing the larvae back and forth between the leaf edges, using them like tiny tubes of glue!

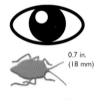

0.7 in.
(18 mm)

Whirligig Beetle

Whirligig beetles are always spinning around and around on the water's surface. They feed on insects that fall into the water, detecting them by the ripples they make. Whirligigs have two pairs of eyes, so they can see above and below the water's surface at the same time. When frightened, the beetles quickly dive underwater. If their enemies are still following, they squirt a cloud of milky liquid to hide their escape.

Wolf Spider

1.18 in. (30 mm)

The wolf spider is a hunter that chases and pounces on its prey, just like a wolf. It has big eyes and very good eyesight. It lives in a silk-lined hole in the ground, only coming out at night to hunt. The female wolf spider carries her egg sac around with her until the eggs hatch. Then the baby spiderlings climb onto her back and travel around with her until they are able to look after themselves.

Fact

Wood ants are valuable pest controllers in woodlands. A colony will kill an average of 6 million caterpillars and other insects in a year.

Wood Ant

0.3 in. (7.6 mm)

The large wood ant's nest is made of leaves, grass stems, and bits of wood. The nest may be several yards high. Inside live around 100,000 ants, ruled over by several queens. Paths lead from the nest to favorite hunting grounds. The ants defend their territory fiercely, squirting acid at their attackers, or biting them.

Xylocopa

(ZIE lo COPE ah)

1 in.
(25.4 mm)

Xylocopa is a carpenter bee. The female bee chews out a nest for her eggs in a hollow twig. First she cuts a tube, and then she places some pollen at the bottom and lays an egg on it—the pollen will be food for the young grub. The bee closes the cell with a mixture of wood shavings and saliva. This wall forms the floor of the next cell, and so on until the bee has a row of up to 16 cells. She stays nearby to guard the nest until the larvae hatch.

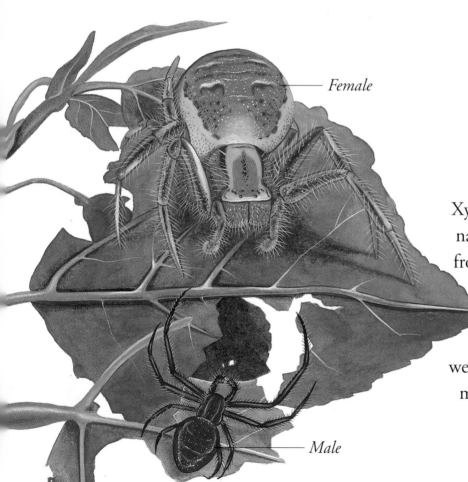

Female

Male

Xytiscus

Female 0.28 in.
(7 mm)

(ZIE TISS cus)

Xytiscus is a small crablike spider, named for its habit of holding its front legs like a crab's pincers and running sideways. It has no web, but lies near the ground waiting for beetles, weevils, and ants. Before the small male mates with the much larger female, he ties her down with a "bridal veil" of silk.

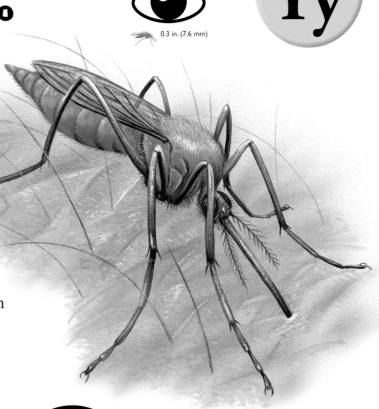

Yellow Fever Mosquito

The yellow fever mosquito is a very dangerous insect—it spreads the disease yellow fever, which it carries in its saliva. The disease is passed to humans as the mosquito bites them. The mosquito breeds in water, even in tiny pools that collect in empty pots. Its eggs can survive over long, dry spells and still hatch when rain eventually falls.

0.3 in. (7.6 mm)

Yucca Moth

(YUCK ah moth)

Wingspan 1.06 in. (27 mm)

The yucca moth lives on yucca plants, found in the deserts of North America and Mexico. It lays its eggs in the flowers, and its caterpillars feed on the plant's seeds. The moth goes to great lengths to make sure her young will have plenty of food. The plant will seed only if it is pollinated with pollen from another flower. To make sure this happens, the moth gathers a ball of pollen from one flower and carefully places it on top of the flower where she will lay her eggs.

Zz

Wingspan
2.95 in. (75 mm)

Zebra Butterfly

The zebra butterfly's bright stripes help hide it from its enemies in the forest. The stripes break up the butterfly's outline, making it hard to spot. The stripes meet at the corner of the wing, which has streamers that look like feelers. Birds mistakenly peck at the wingtips instead of its head, causing less damage and giving the butterfly a chance to escape.

Zygaenid

(ZIE gee NID)

Wingspan
1.38 in. (35 mm)

Zygaenid or burnet moths fly by day. Their striking red markings warn enemies, such as birds, that they are poisonous. The moths' caterpillars feed on poisonous ragweed, taking in the plant's poisons. They keep the poisons even when they turn into adult moths. Once a bird has tasted a poisonous zygaenid moth and felt sick, it will recognize others and avoid them.

Glossary

Abdomen Rear section of the body of an insect or spider. It contains the stomach, gut, and organs.

Antenna (plural antennae) A feeler: a thin whiplike or hairlike structure that a bug uses to feel, smell, or hear things. Antennae come in pairs, one on each side of the top of the head, behind the eyes.

Arachnid An arthropod with eight legs—spiders, scorpions, ticks, and mites are all arachnids.

Arthropod A bug with no backbone but with a hard outer layer (exoskeleton).

Camouflage Shape, color, and pattern that help an animal blend in with its background, so that its enemies—and its prey—cannot see it easily.

Caterpillar The larva of a moth or butterfly.

Cell Found in the nest of a bee or wasp, a little "cup" formed of wax, mud, or paper, in which the insect stores its eggs, larvae, pupae, or food.

Chamber Roomlike section of a nest of ants or termites. There are nursery and food chambers, and the royal chamber, where the queen lives.

Chrysalis (plural chrysalids) A hard case inside which the caterpillar changes into an adult butterfly or moth.

Cocoon A silk case that protects the eggs of a spider or the pupa of an insect.

Colony A large group of creatures of the same kind, such as ants or termites, that live together.

Courtship Animal behavior that leads to choosing a mate and mating.

Drone A male bee who mates with the queen but does not do any work in the colony.

Egg sac A silk bag that a female spider spins around her eggs to protect them.

Exoskeleton The hard outer layer of a bug. The exoskeleton protects the soft insides and provides a frame on which the muscles can pull to move the bug's limbs.

Fungus (plural fungi) Simple living things that grow rapidly, like mold, mildew, and mushrooms, and feed on rotting plant and animal material. Some ants "farm" fungi in their colonies for food.

Grub Sometimes used to describe wormlike larvae.

Host An animal that supports and feeds a parasite.

Insect A bug whose body is made up of three sections, with three pairs of legs joined to the middle section and one pair of feelers on its head. Adult insects usually have one or two pairs of wings.

Joints Hinges between the sections of limbs, feelers, and mouthparts that allow them to bend.

Larva (plural larvae) A young bug that looks very different from its parents. The grubs of bees and beetles, and the caterpillars of butterflies and moths, are larvae.

Mating The coming together of male and female animals to produce young.

Metamorphosis The change in shape and color that takes place when a young bug changes into an adult. Dragonflies, butterflies, and mosquitoes go through metamorphosis.

Glossary

Mimicry Copying the shape or color of another animal or an object, so enemies do not notice the creature.

Molting The shedding of the hard outer layer of the exoskeleton, or "skin," of a bug as it grows bigger. The new layer underneath is soft at first, so the bug can expand.

Mouthparts The mouths of bugs. They are made of the same hard material as the exoskeleton. The mouthparts of bugs are made up of pairs of jointed paddlelike structures that form jaws or scoops. Some mouthparts are sharp-pointed tubes for piercing plant stems; others have sawlike edges for chewing leaves or fangs for injecting poison.

Nectar The sweet-scented sugary liquid found at the base of the petals in a flower.

Nymph A young insect that is like a small version of its parents, and changes step by step into an adult.

Organ Part of an animal's body that does a special job. For example, the heart is an organ that pumps blood around the body.

Paralyze To make an animal unable to move.

Parasite An animal that lives in or on another animal, feeding on it and giving nothing in return.

Pincers A pair of limbs that work together to grip something tightly between them. Pincers always act together—each limb moves toward or away from the other one by the same amount.

Poison A substance that can cause injury, sickness, or even death.

Pollen The yellow, orange, or red powder inside a flower. It contains the flower's male reproductive cells. To form seeds, a flower must receive pollen from another flower. This is called pollination. Pollen is carried from flower to flower by insects or by the wind.

Predator An animal that hunts and eats other animals.

Prey An animal that is hunted and eaten by another animal.

Queen In most colonies of bees, wasps, ants, and termites, the queen is the only female that produces young. She is much bigger than the other insects. Swollen with eggs, she spends her whole life laying eggs, while the other members of the colony (the workers) feed her and keep her clean. The queen gives off a special scent that keeps the workers happy so they don't fight or try to take her place.

Rival Usually a male bug that competes with another male for a female to mate with.

Saliva A clear liquid made in the mouth that helps digest food.

Sap A liquid found in plants.

Silk Threads made by spiders and some insects.

Wingspan Distance from the tip of one wing to the tip of the other wing when the wings are spread out. It is a measure of the size of a winged insect or bird.

Worker Most of the insects in a colony of bees, wasps, ants, or termites are called workers. They gather food for the colony, feed and clean the young, look after the queen, and keep the nest clean. The workers do not usually breed.

Index

Index